MOON-WHALES

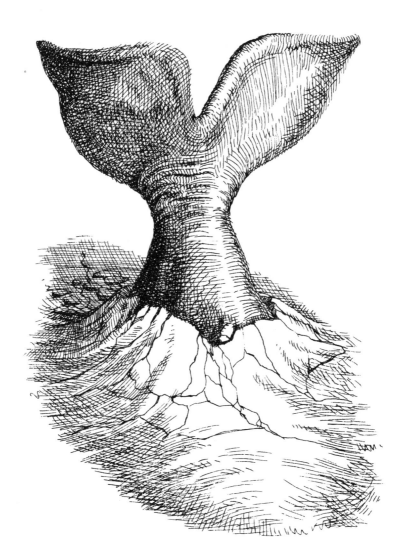

KU-170-183

Also by Ted Hughes

for children
MEET MY FOLKS!
FFANGS THE VAMPIRE BAT AND THE KISS OF TRUTH
WHAT IS THE TRUTH?
A Farmyard Fable for the Young
(Winner of the *Guardian* Award for Children's Fiction
and the Signal Poetry Award)
UNDER THE NORTH STAR
SEASON SONGS
THE EARTH OWL AND OTHER MOON-PEOPLE
HOW THE WHALE BECAME
THE IRON MAN: A Story in Five Nights
(Winner of the Kurt Maschler Award)
NESSIE, THE MANNERLESS MONSTER
THE COMING OF THE KINGS and other plays

POETRY IN THE MAKING
An Anthology of Poems and Programmes
from *Listening and Writing*

for adults
THE HAWK IN THE RAIN
LUPERCAL
WODWO
CROW
GAUDETE
CAVE BIRDS
REMAINS OF ELMET
RIVER
MOORTOWN
FLOWERS AND INSECTS
SELECTED POEMS 1957–1981
SELECTED POEMS (with Thom Gunn)

SENECA'S OEDIPUS
adapted by Ted Hughes
A CHOICE OF SHAPESKEARE'S VERSE
edited by Ted Hughes
THE RATTLE BAG
edited by Ted Hughes and Seamus Heaney

MOON-WHALES
Ted Hughes
illustrated by Chris Riddell

s/166848

WEXFORD
COUNTY
LIBRARY.

faber and faber
LONDON · BOSTON

First published in the USA in 1976
First published in Britain in this revised edition 1988
by Faber and Faber Limited
3 Queen Square, London WC1N 3AU

Photoset by Parker Typesetting Service Leicester
Printed in Great Britain by
Redwood Burn Ltd Trowbridge Wiltshire
All rights reserved

© Ted Hughes, 1963, 1976, 1988
Illustrations © Chris Riddell, 1988

British Library Cataloguing in Publication Data

Hughes, Ted
Moon-whales: and other moon poems.
I. Title   II. Riddell, Chris
821'.914   PR6058.U37
ISBN 0-571-14742-9

For Frieda and Nicholas

Contents

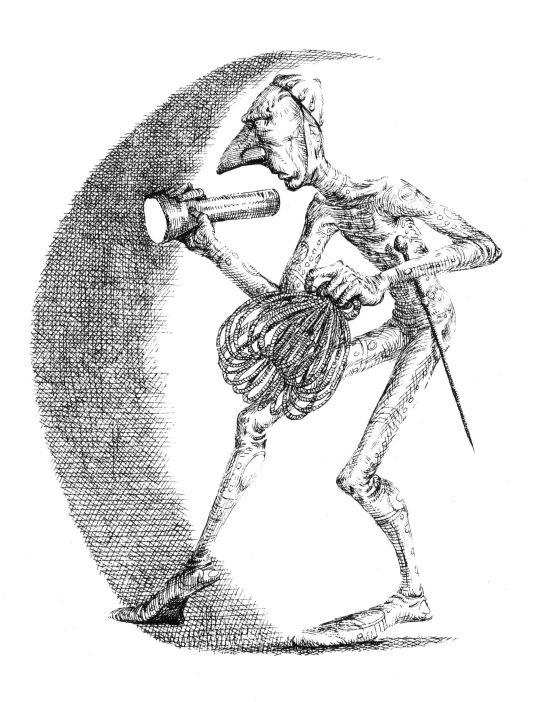

Moon-Whales

They plough through the moon stuff
Just under the surface
Lifting the moon's skin
Like a muscle
But so slowly it seems like a lasting mountain
Breathing so rarely it seems like a volcano
Leaving a hole blasted in the moon's skin

Sometimes they plunge deep
Under the moon's plains
Making their magnetic way
Through the moon's interior metals
Sending the astronaut's instruments scatty.

Their music is immense
Each note hundreds of years long
Each whole tune a moon-age

So they sing to each other unending songs
As unmoving they move their immovable masses

Their eyes closed ecstatic

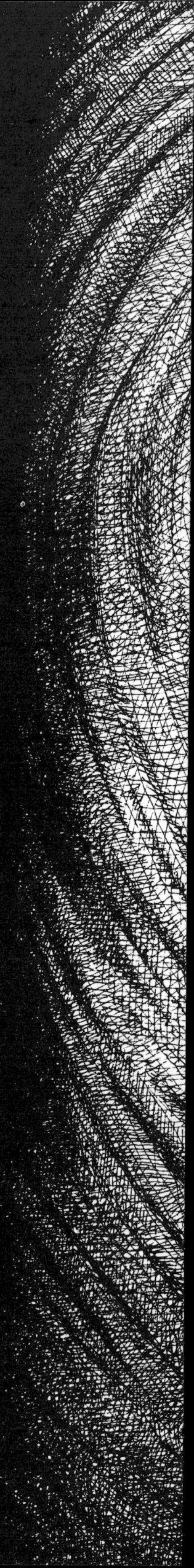

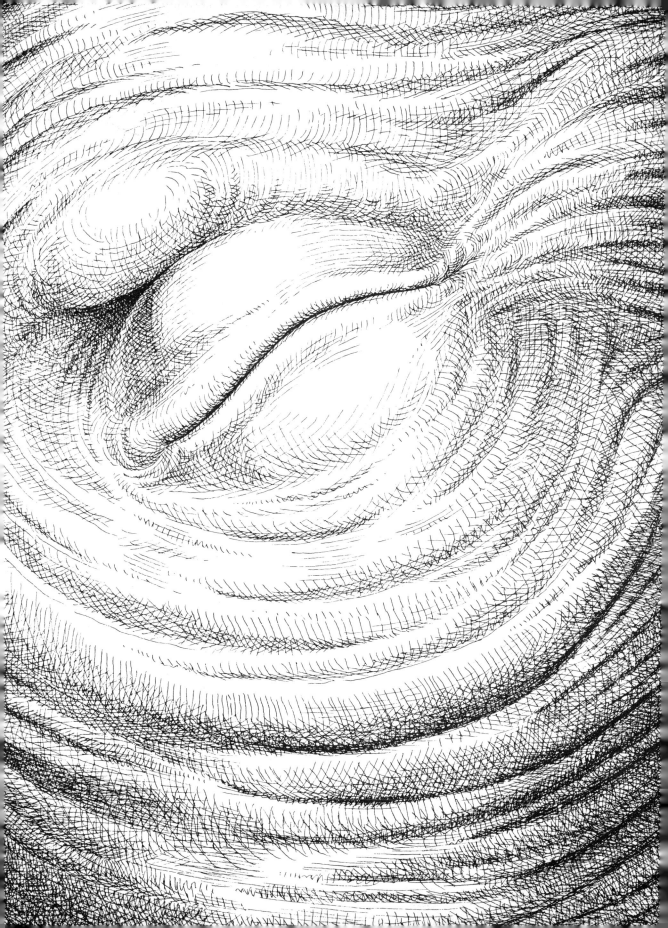

A Moon-Lily

Marvellously white is the moon-lily.
But that is not all, O no, not nearly.

When it has reached its full height
But before its swelling bud shows any white

You think you hear a ghost inside your house –
It whispers and titters, so it is not a mouse.

By next night it is a happy humming.
Now go look at your lily, you will see a split of white petal coming.

Next night it is a singing – very far
But very clear and sweet, and wherever you are

The voice is always in some other room.
Down in the garden, your lily is in bloom.

For days now, while your flower stands full and proud,
That strange lady's singing, gentle and happy, and never very loud,

Comes and goes in your house, and all night long.
Till one night – suddenly – weeping. Something is wrong!

And you know, down in your garden, before you go
The lily has started to fade, there is brown on her snow.

Then come nights of quiet sobbing, and no sleep for you,
Till your lily's withering is quite through.

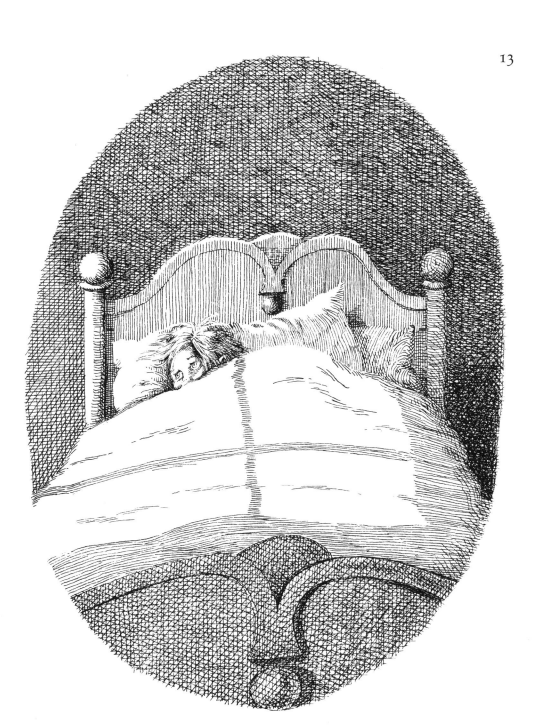

The Burrow Wolf

A kind of wolf lives in the moon's holes
Waiting for meteorites to score goals.

The meteorites come down blazing with velocity
And this wolf greets them with a huge grin of ferocity.

Whack to the back of his gullet go those glowing rocks
And the wolf's eyes start clean out of his head on eleven-inch stalks.

But only for a moment, then he smiles and swallows
And shuts his eyes as over the melt of marshmallows.

Rockets nosediving on to the moon for modern adventures
Will have to reckon with those abnormal dentures.

Many a spaceman in the years to come
Will be pestled with meteorites in that horny tum.

If he does not dive direct into those jaws
He may well wander in there after a short pause.

For over the moon general madness reigns –
Bad when the light waxes, worse when it wanes –

And he might lunatically mistake this wolf for his wife.
So the man in the moon ended *his* life.

In every moon-mirror lurks a danger.
Look in it – and there glances out some stranger
Who stares at you astounded and goes pale,
Probably gurgles dumbstruck, or utters a wail
And flees, as if he had met a ghost –
And the mirror once more is a hole of silver mist.

Another time you glance in it and see
Strange faces, crowding excitedly,
As if you were some monster on display
And they could look at you, having had to pay,
Through that small window, from which they are pushed
By other amazed faces, that stare, hushed.

Or washing your face, you look – and see your face
Instantly shouldered out of place
By crowds of stricken faces from long ago,
Faces full of pleading and woe,
Who reach hands toward you, crying dumb,
But are shoved aside by others who come
Crying out of the future, baby faces
Strong as giants, with Martian grimaces,
Trying to burst and scatter the mirror frame –
What if they *did* burst it? What if they came?

Banish them, quick, with an angry frown
And turn the mirror face-down.

Moon-Thirst

Moon-thirst
Is the worst.

Moon-stroke
Makes you croak.

A mighty smite
Of Moonlight

Turns your playful soul
That played like a silly foal

Into a load
Of dark toad.

He squats under a rock
Like a stopped clock.

'A drink! O for a drink!'
He croaks, with dusty blink.

'Ah, how low I have sunk
Since the moon made me drunk!'

But then, with raptures in his eyes,
He sees the moon rise.

Once more, with awful lust,
He plods out into the dust.

The Moon-Oak

The Moon-oak
Is a sort of vegetable hawk.
He carries the Moon in his feet
Because that is his meat.
He reaches his arms high through the starry night
And that is his great flight
Long ago begun –

He flies toward the Sun
Because that is his nest.
There he will rest
And there greet his mate
Who brings the Earth in her feet.

Then Earth and Moon will expire
Among their nestlings of fire.

S/166848

WEXFORD
COUNTY
LIBRARY.

The Moon-Haggis

The moon-haggis has a crazy
Cruel hiccup, as it flees
Across rugged highlands and flat oozy
Lowlands like a bagpipe with knees.

It skirls and careens its passion
To the hag-thorn and to the crone-stone
And to the black loch without a fish in,
Droning its chanter and chanting its drone.

Till a wild highlander, deserting his bottle,
With dirk and with dag
Cuts its throttle
And eats its bag.

Then the moon in the sky
Lets a gurgling cry
And shrinks to the skin
That the haggis lived in.

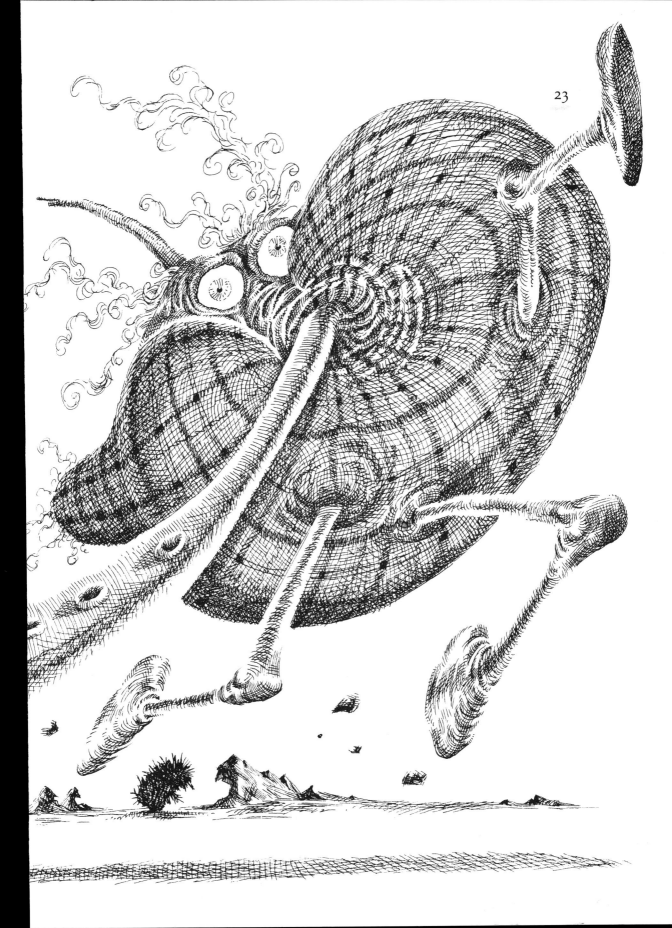

Moon-Wings

Unexpectedly descending things
Are these moon-wings.

Broad, soft, silent and white
And like a huge barn-owl's is their flight.

They veer and eddy and swoop,
They loop the alarming loop,

No head or limbs or body – just wings.
A pair pounces down on you and clings –

You feel them trying to grow
Into your shoulder blades, then they flap and you go

You go you go you go –
Where or which way you can never know.

High over goggling faces you are swung –
And just as unexpectedly suddenly flung

Down to the ground – after flying
Nine or ten miles without trying,

Then the wings just whirl off
With a sort of whiffling laugh.

I tried the bell-pull –
But what use is the silk-tassel tail of a white bull?

I went in, feeling watched.
But it hadn't hatched.

I climbed the stair
That died in the cellar.

I opened the little door –
Space sat smiling there.

I slipped into the attic
Just as it turned over and the sand started to pour back.

I looked into the mirror –
It escaped, leaving a big-eyed feather.

I looked into the inkwell
Which still hadn't set sail.

When I met her in the dark
She jabbed me with a bent hypodermic.

Was I juggling with hoops?
Was I hanging from a hook through my lips?

I woke up in the tower

And there the moon, molten silver in a great cauldron,
Was being poured
Through the eye of a needle

Spun on to bobbins and sold to poets
For sewing their eyelids together
So they can sing better.

Moon-Shadow Beggars

Crossing the frontier from dark to light
You pass the shadows, some of which bite
Because they need your blood, some on one leg
Hobble beside you and merely beg.
You can't hear what it is they want you to give –
I'll tell you, it is the body in which you live.
They cling with fingers that have no strength,
They reach after you with arms of elastic length,
They screech, sob and suffer in a dreadful way.
Be resolute, pass them without delay.
For if you pity them, and pause, you will stay
Caught among them forever, they will pour
Into you through the wide open door
Of your eye-pupil, and fill you up
And you will be nothing but a skinful of shadows
Whispering shadow-talk and groping for
The well-known handle of your own front door
With fingers that cannot feel it.
It is a horrible state and nothing can heal it.

The Earth-Owl

Far undergrounded,
Moon-miners dumbfounded
Hear the speed-whistle
Of this living missile
As he tears through the strata
Or splits apart a
Subterrene Gibraltar,
His wings do not falter
At deposits of iron –
He just screws a new eye on
The end of his skull
Which is shaped with great skill
As a terrible drill
That revolves on his neck –
His spine is the spindle,
His body the handle,
His wings are the thrust –
In a gunshot of dust
Sparks, splinters and all he
Bursts from the mine-wall,
Shrieking, 'Ek, Ek!'
And crashing straight on
Is instantly gone.

When he has dined, the man-eating tiger leaves certain signs.
But nothing betrays the moon's hideous number nines.
Nobody knows where they sleep off their immense meals.
They strike so fatally nobody knows how one feels.
One-eyed, one-legged, they start out of the ground with such a shout
The chosen victim's eyes instantly fall out.
They do not leave so much as a hair but smack their chops
And go off thinner than ever with grotesque hops.

Now the shark will take a snack by shearing off half a swimmer.
Over the moon presides a predator even grimmer.
Descending without warning from the interstellar heavens
Whirling like lathes, arrive the fearful horde of number sevens.
Whatever they touch, whether owl or elephant, poet or scientist,
The wretched victim wilts instantly to a puff of purple mist
And before he can utter a cry or say goodbye to kith and kin
Those thin-gut number sevens have sucked him ravenously in.

Mosquitoes seem dreadful, for they drink at a man as he sleeps.
Night and day over the moon a far craftier horror creeps.
It is hard to know what species of creature you would have to be
To escape the attentions of the moon's horrible number three.
He attacks as a nightmare, and the sleeper dreams he is being turned
    inside out
And sucked dry like an orange, and when he wakes it has all come
    about.
Ever afterwards he is perfectly hollow and dry, while his precious
    insides
Nourish some gross number three wherever that monster now resides.

But the thing that specializes in hunting down the great hero
Is the flying strangler, the silent zero.
It is luckily quite rare, perhaps there is only one.
According to legend it lives sleepily coiled around the sun.
But when a moon-hero appears it descends and hovers just over his
    head.
His enemies call it a halo, but his friends see it and tremble with dread.
And sure enough, in the very best of his days,
That zero drops around his neck, tightens, and whirls away with him
    into the sun's blaze.

Moon-Wind

There is no wind on the moon at all
    Yet things get blown about.
In utter utter stillness
    Your candle shivers out.

In utter utter stillness
    A giant marquee
Booms and flounders past you
    Like a swan at sea.

In utter utter stillness
    While you stand in the street
A squall of hens and cabbages
    Knocks you off your feet.

In utter utter stillness
    While you stand agog
A tearing twisting sheet of pond
    Clouts you with a frog.

A camp of caravans suddenly
    Squawks and takes off.
A ferris wheel bounds along the skyline
    Like a somersaulting giraffe.

Roots and foundations, nails and screws,
    Nothing holds fast,
Nothing can resist the moon's
    Dead-still blast.

Tulips on the moon are a kind of military band.
A bed of crimson ones will march up to your window and take its
stand.
Then out of their flashing brass and silver they rip some Prussian
fanfare.
Nobody asked them, and nobody takes any notice of their blare.
After a while, they about turn and to kettledrums goose-step away.
Soon under somebody else's window they are presenting the same
deafening bouquet.

Moon-Nasturtiums

Nasturtiums on earth are small and seething with horrible green
    caterpillars.
On the moon they are giant, jungles of them, and swarming with noisy
    gorillas.
And the green caterpillars there are the size of anacondas.
The butterflies that hatch from those are one of the moon's greatest
    wonders.
Though few survive the depredations of the gorillas
Who are partial to the succulent huge eggs that produce such
    caterpillars.

Moon-Dog-Daisies

Dog-daisies on the moon run in packs
And it is their habit to carry moon-bees on their backs.
Dog-daisies live mainly on the small squealing sounders of sow-thistles
That charge about the moon's canyons, and the daisies are not deterred
   by their bristles.
When a sow-thistle has given up the ghost to the daisy-dogs
Those moon-bees pounce down on to the feast and make themselves
   hogs.

Moon-Hops

Hops are a menace on the moon, a nuisance crop.
From hilltop to hilltop they hop hopelessly without stop.
Nobody knows what they want to find, they just go on till they drop,
Clip-clop at first, then flip-flop, then slip-slop, till finally they droopily
 drop and all their pods pop.

Moon-Heads

Shining like lamps and light as balloons
Bodiless heads drift and bump among the moon's

Volcanoes, each like a demon-ghost,
A paper Chinese lantern kite that has got lost –

Except they are not made of paper O no,
They are made of astral light colder than any snow

And they are not ghosts – they never lived at all.
They are the spirit-shapes of unborn prehistoric monsters still awaiting
   the Creator's call,

Still waiting to be properly born and given bodies of flesh.
To walk about and eat and sleep and be normal is their only wish.

But they fear they are too late,
They fear they are out of date,

And they are probably right,
Therefore they gnash their fangs and shriek in the face of the lonely
   wayfarer at dead of night.

Music on the Moon

The pianos on the moon are so long
The pianist's hand must be fifteen fingers strong.

The violins on the moon are so violent
They have to be sunk in deep wells, and then they only seem to be
  silent.

The bassoons on the moon blow no notes
But huge blue loons that flap slowly away with undulating throats.

Now harmonicas on the moon are humorous,
The tunes produce German Measles, but the speckles more numerous.

Of a trumpet on the moon you can never hear enough
Because it puffs the trumpeter up like a balloon and he floats off.

Double basses on the moon are a risk all right,
At the first note enormous black hands appear and carry away
  everything in sight.

Even a triangle on the moon is risky,
One ping – and there's your head a half bottle of Irish whisky.

In the same way, be careful with the flute –
Because wherever he is, your father will find himself converted into a
  disgusting old boot.

On the whole it's best to stick to the moon's drums.
Whatever damage they do is so far off in space the news never comes.

Moon-Ways

The moon's roads are treacherous.
It's no good taking a bus.
The road that takes you home loyally
Year after year, suddenly cruelly
Runs you to jail instead.
Too late to shake your head
When the cell-door clangs shut.
Home is where you're put.

A road that had always led to your friends
One day abruptly ends
In a ghost-town –
Ceilings coming down,
Brambles in hallways, owls' nests in beds,
Mouldy playing cards, dolls' heads.

Some roads, more active, stray
Somewhere fresh every day –
Even from minute to minute.
A village so close that you are all but in it
Suddenly it's a lake –

You feel the road ripple like a snake
As it changes its mind.

Better leave roads behind.
Better just train your nose
And go as a bee goes.

The Snail of the Moon

Saddest of all things on the moon is the snail without a shell.
You locate him by his wail, a wail heartrending and terrible

Which sounds as though something had punctured him.
His battle for progress is both slow and grim.

He is sad, wet and cold, like a huge tear
In a thin skin. He wanders far and near

Searching for a shelter from the sun –
For the first sun-beam will melt and make him run.

So moving in moon-dark only he must keep going,
With muscles rippling and saliva flowing,

But nowhere on the moon is there garage
For such a snail. He is not merely large

He is over a mile from side to side.
It's useless him seeking any place to hide.

So wailingly and craning his periscopes
Over the dark bulge of the moon he gropes.

He has searched every inch of the moon. I guess
That silver is snail-saliva silveriness.

Crab-Grass

When you get to the moon, watch out for crab-grass.
It is in complete control of the moon's badlands, alas.

It drives the foolish gooseberries in fat gaggling flocks
Over high cliffs so that they split and lie helplessly edible below on the
   rocks.

It herds the moon-potatoes through their great seas of volcanic ash
And nips their flippers so they leap ashore and flounder where they
   cannot so much as splash.

When a crab-grass comes upon a benighted tourist,
Of five hundred possible ends he may meet, that is the surest.

A crab-grass is ginger and hairy, and usually moves about six inches
   per year
In hordes of up to ten million, but that is its bottom gear.

You know a crab-grass is about to attack, by its excited hoot.
It has no eyes, so do not wait to see the whites of those before you
   shoot.

The moon is a dusty place
But it's no good trying to sweep the dust up.
All the witches burned at the stake on earth
In the wicked times when that was a sport,
All those witches who worshipped the moon
Sent their scorched souls there to cool off.
So there they all are, living in the crannies
And looking exactly like cockroaches.
To all appearances they are in fact cockroaches,
Except they have a passion for brooms.
They forget what it is about brooms
So important to witches,
But they remember they are very important.
Seeing a broom, they become frantic,
They salivate, their tiny eyes swivel on stalks,
But all cockroaches can do is eat,
So they rush passionately at the broom
And passionately they devour it
Right down to the stick.

Then they zig-zag away frustrated,
Reminded of something important they cannot remember,
Splinters in their teeth and their eyes full of dust.

The Moon-Hyena

The moon-hyena's laughter
Emerges at midnight or soon after
From a volcano's holes.
Its echo tumbles and rolls.
It grows like a moon quake, always louder , never softer, horrible
  laughter,

A laughter of dark hell,
Mad laughter of a skull,
Coming to devour the living ones.
You are wakened by the scare in your bones.
The moon-hyena is abroad, it is coming over the hill.

And it seems to you as you waken
The whole moon is being shaken
By its own ghastly amusement –
A crazy, cruel laughter, spreading amazement.

But then, just in time, you recall
The moon-hyena is not dangerous at all.
In spite of its moon-size terrific voice
It is about the size of a mouse
With a furry powder-puff tail.

And nobody is more distressed
By the laughter that erupts from its chest
Instead of sweet song, when it tries to sing,
Than this tiny creature, creeping along –

Yet it is so full of love and joy that sing it must, or bust.

Mushrooms on the Moon

Mushrooms on the moon are delicious.
But those who eat them become birds, beasts, or fishes.
Space-fishes, space-beasts, and space-birds.
They stray out into space in shoals and flocks and herds.

At first, rapturous and excited,
But suddenly feeling space all round them and above and below they
   are affrighted.

Then goggling space-fish go fleeting in formations,
Space-beasts go trailing here and there in endless migrations,
Space-birds go hurtling from one end of space to the other in endless
   agitations
Among the constellations.

But space is too vast, they are lost, as if quite blind.
They are looking for the human bodies they left behind

On the tiny tiny moon, so tiny, tiny as a dust-grain

Which they can never hope to alight on again.

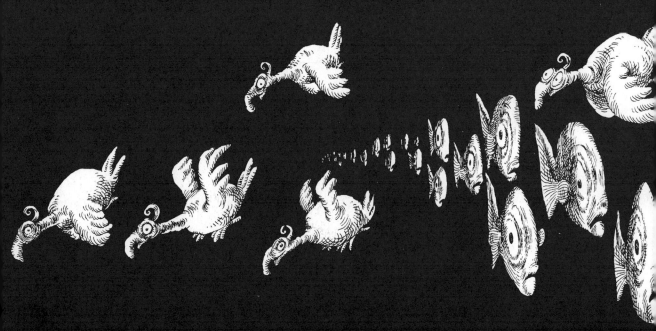

The Adaptable
Mountain Dugong

The Mountain Dugong is a simply fantastic animal.
It lives mainly in extinct volcanoes, uttering its lonely call
Which nobody answers, because it is the sole Mountain Dugong, there
    are no others at all.

It keeps alive with a number of surprising tricks.
It looks like a table, just as a stick insect looks like sticks.
So nobody interferes, they think it's an old table dumped there by
    passing hicks.

But lo, what is under that most common-looking table?
Spare heads and legs in great assortment, all looking very much alive
    and able.
The Mountain Dugong is its own Noah's Ark, and he will not be stuck
    with any one label.

For instance, here comes a pack of wild dogs, each with a mouth like a
    refuse bin.
They have smelt the Mountain Dugong's peculiar fried fish smell and
    want to get their teeth in,
Because wild dogs need to devour every living thing in all directions
    and to them this is no sin.

But the Mountain Dugong is already prepared, the wild dogs cannot
    shock it.
He unscrews his table-legs and screws a greyhound leg into each socket
And is away over the crater-edge with all his equipment in three leaps
    like a rubber rocket.

The wild dogs begin to wear him down, they head him in a circle,
    they bring him to a stop, they gather in a ring,
But all this time the Mountain Dugong has not been malingering.
He has screwed on to himself the headpiece of a tiger and in no time
    those wild dogs are a pile of chewed string.

This is how the adaptable Mountain Dugong carries on without loss.
He will screw on reindeer feet and head where there is nothing but
    Arctic moss.
Where there is nothing but sand the legs and hump of a camel soon get
    him across.

And he is forced to such tricks because there will never be another of
    his sort.
He has to keep himself in circulation by means no sane traveller would
    report.
I record his habits here, in case he should never again be seen or
    caught.

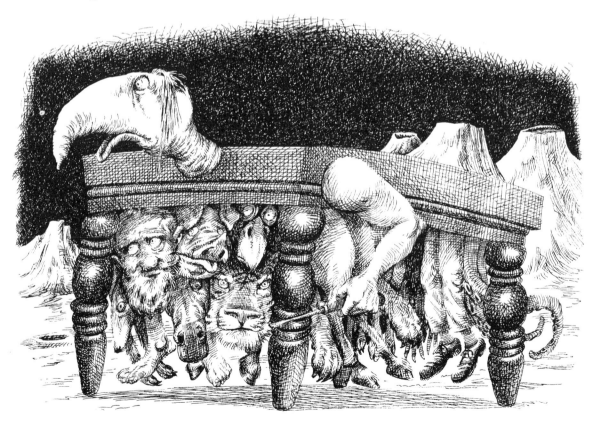

Moon-Cloud Gripe

Moon-cloud gripe first shows
By a whitening of the nose.
Then your hair begins to stir,
Your eyes begin to blur.
Then you go blue,
You shiver and say 'Flu.'
Then between your fingertips
A blue spark skips.
Then an amazing red
Zag zigs up from your head
And splits the ceiling.
You have the feeling
You are going to explode.
You are rumbling like a road
Under a ten-ton wagon.
Then a long orange dragon
Like a rip-saw tears
From your mouth and flares
The furniture to ash.
Down you crash.
The walls split and shake.
Neighbours shout 'Earthquake!'
(How can they tell
It's just that you're not well?)

The only cure, they say,
Is to sigh for a whole day.

Tree-Disease

On the moon with great ease
You can catch tree-disease.
The symptoms are birds
Seeming interested in your words
And examining your ears.
Then a root peers
From under the nail
Of your big toe, then
You'd better get cured quick
Or you'll be really sick.

I hope you never contract
The lunar galloping cact-
us, which is when dimples
Suddenly turn to pimples,
And these pimples bud –
Except for the odd dud –
Each one into a head with hair
And a face just like the one you wear.
These heads grow pea-size to begin
From your brows, your nose, your cheeks and your chin.
But soon enough they're melon-size,
All with mouths and shining eyes.
Within five days your poor neck spreads
A bunch of ten or fifteen heads
All hungry, arguing or singing
(Somewhere under your own head's ringing).
And so for one whole tedious week
You must admit you are a freak.

And then, perhaps when you gently cough
For silence, one of the heads drops off.
Their uproar instantly comes to a stop.
Then in silence, plop by plop,
With eyes and mouth most firmly closed,
Your rival heads, in turn deposed,
Land like pumpkins round your feet.
You walk on feeling light and neat.

In the next mirror are assured
That now you stand completely cured.

Moon-Weapons

There are weapons on the moon
Which behave oddly.
They appear, lying handy,
Near the ungodly.

The ungodly, he loves all weapons,
And when he meets one such
He just can't resist it.
He has to touch.

If it's a sword,
He strokes its moony blade,
And his eyes close with pleasure.
But it is moon-made.

And the next thing
The sword's evil spirit
Stares from that man's eyes
Red as a ferret.

And he is moon-mad
Till he stabs somebody –
Then moonier and madder
He laughs all bloody.

Then the sword chuckles and flees
On a hellish blast –
Leaving one dead man
And one man aghast.

Cabbages on the moon are not cabbages.
They are little old women, gabbing old baggages.

Where our cabbages are bundles of leaves, gently flip-flapping,
Those are bundles of great loose lips, yappity-yap-yapping.

Yappity-yap, yappity-yap, yappity-yap-yap-yap!
Where our cabbages have hearts, those have gossip gushing out of a
     gap.

Not all of them are just bundles of lips. It appears
Some are in fact bundles of flapping ears, just like bundles of small
     elephant ears.

Flappity-flap, flappity-flap, flappity-flap-flap-flap!
Our cabbages are worn out by caterpillars, but those get ragged on
     sheer yap.

So some are all yap and some are all ears and their mutual amusements
     resound.
And they are so tough they can go on at that till their one scaly old
     shank grows right down into the ground.

Moon Art

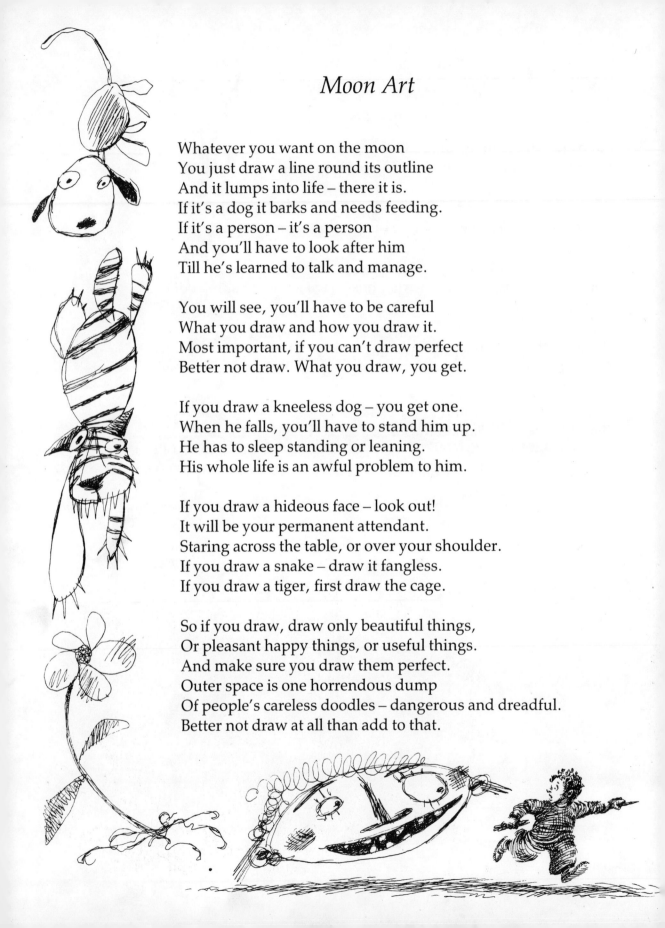

Whatever you want on the moon
You just draw a line round its outline
And it lumps into life – there it is.
If it's a dog it barks and needs feeding.
If it's a person – it's a person
And you'll have to look after him
Till he's learned to talk and manage.

You will see, you'll have to be careful
What you draw and how you draw it.
Most important, if you can't draw perfect
Better not draw. What you draw, you get.

If you draw a kneeless dog – you get one.
When he falls, you'll have to stand him up.
He has to sleep standing or leaning.
His whole life is an awful problem to him.

If you draw a hideous face – look out!
It will be your permanent attendant.
Staring across the table, or over your shoulder.
If you draw a snake – draw it fangless.
If you draw a tiger, first draw the cage.

So if you draw, draw only beautiful things,
Or pleasant happy things, or useful things.
And make sure you draw them perfect.
Outer space is one horrendous dump
Of people's careless doodles – dangerous and dreadful.
Better not draw at all than add to that.

Moon-Thorns

The Moon's thorns
Are corkscrew curved horns
Waiting in a bush
To make a startling rush
And stab you to the bone.
While you groan
A drop of your blood
Soaks in where you stood.

From that tiny mote of moon-mud
Pokes a tiny bud.
It strengthens, it grows,
It opens a surprising face
And that is the moon-rose
Famed throughout space.

The horned bloom given
At marriages in heaven.

Moon-Ravens

Are silver white
Like the moonlight
And their croak, their bark
Is not dark
And ominous,
But luminous
And a sweet chime
Always announcing time
For good news to come
If there is some,
And if there isn't
Then there's a moon-present –
That is, a stillness,
And if you have any illness
It flits out of your mouth
In the shape of a black moth

Which the moon-raven then follows
And swallows.

Moon-Marriage

Marriage on the moon is rather strange.
It's nothing you can arrange.

You dream a frog comes in shivering from the moon-snow
And clings to you crying: 'O!O!O!
I am so happy you married me!'
You wake up frozen blue, and need a stiff brandy –
Lucky you, if you have one handy.

Or maybe a smiling wolf comes up close
While you doze off, in your chair, and gives you a kiss,
A cold wet doggy kiss, and then you know
You have been CHOSEN, and it's no good flailing awake bawling, 'No!'
Wherever the wolf is, she just goes on smiling –
It's an eerie feeling.

Or maybe deep in your sleep a mountain looms
With rumbling and lightning and misty glooms,
Whispering, 'Do you love me
As much as I love you?' And you wake
With your nose bleeding, and all one terrible ache
Like a worn-out mountaineer,
And still feeling the precipices near.

But there's no telling what bride
May choose you from the inside.

And if you're a girl you're no better off.

Before somebody normal can make you his wife
A Siberian tiger snatches you up in your sleep
And carries you to his cave under the glacier.
Then when you wake, while you dress and comb your hair,
And even long after, when you go out shopping,
You have only to close your eyes and you hear
Your tiger breathing near.
Woe betide any man then who enters your house.
He will be removed by your abnormal spouse.

If you're lucky you might be picked by a little bird, such as a swallow,
An undemanding fellow,
Who clears off six months in the year on a world hike
Leaving you to do as you like.

On the moon it is all a matter of luck
Is marriage.

And the only offspring are poems.

The Moon-Mourner

The moon is haunted by a crying
Sobbing crying groaning crying

Person that you cannot see –
He cries, cries heartrendingly

Night or day no difference,
The wailing gibberish makes no sense,

Crying sadder than ever you heard
As if the end of the world had occurred

And now the news has reached the moon.
As it approaches you almost swoon,

As it comes close you almost drop.
On and on without a stop

And louder and louder and closer until
You think the fright of it might kill.

And now you think it has come for you.
There is nothing you can do.

And it is right inside you now.
But then it's passed, you don't know how.

You were a puddle it had to wade.
And slowly away you hear it fade

Among the craters white as snow
With its petrifying woe.

The Dracula Vine

People on the moon love a pet.
But there's only one pet you can get –
The Dracula Vine, a monstrous sight!
But the moon-people like it all right.

This pet looks like a climbing plant
Made from parts of elephant.
But each flower is a hippo's head
Endlessly gaping to be fed.

Now this pet eats everything –
Whatever you can shovel or fling.
It snaps up all your old cardboard boxes
Your empty cans and your stuffed foxes.

And wonder of wonders! The very flower
You have given something to devour
Sprouts on the spot a luscious kind of pear
Without pips, and you can eat it there.

So this is a useful pet
And loyal if well-treat.
But if you treat it badly
It will wander off sadly

Till somebody with more garbage than you
Gives its flowers something to do.

The Armies of the Moon

Many as the troubles upon the old moon are,
The worst is its unending Civil War.

The soldiers of the Moon-Dark are round and small.
Each clanks like a tank, blue armour covering all.
He wears asbestos overalls under his clatter.
So if he's thrown to the volcanoes it does not matter.
His weapon is a sackful of bloodsucking vampires
(Wars on the moon are without rules or umpires).
He flings these bats one at a time into the enemy host.
When it returns full he sends it to the first aid post
Where it gives up the blood for transfusions later in the battle.
Then it flies back to its owner with renewed mettle.

The soldiers of the Moon-Light are tall and thin.
They seem to be glisteningly naked, but are in fact silvered with tin.
They are defensive fighters, but pretty hot –
Their armament is an electric torch and a lobsterpot.
They flash their beam into the vampire's eyes and so puzzle it.
Then cram the lobsterpot on to its head, and so muzzle it.
They long for the last great battle in which they will catch
Every vampire the Moon-Darkers have been able to hatch.
Then they will rush upon the helpless Moon-Darkers and soon
With knitting-needles abolish them forever from the face of the moon.

The Silent Eye

On the moon lives an eye.
It flies about in the sky,
Staring, glaring, or just peering.
You can't see what it uses for steering.
It is about the size of a large owl,
But has no feathers, and so is by no means a fowl.
Sometimes it zips overhead from horizon to horizon,
Then you know it has seen something surprisin'.
Mostly it hovers just above you and stares
Rudely down into your most private affairs.
Nobody minds it much, they say it has charm.
It has no mouth or hands, so how could it do harm?
Besides, as I say, it has these appealing ways.
When you are sitting sadly under crushing dismays,
This eye floats up and gazes at you like a mourner,
Then droops and wilts and a huge tear sags from its corner,
And soon it is sobbing and expressing such woe
You begin to wish it would stop it and just go.

A Moon-Witch

A moon-witch is no joke.
She comes as a sort of smoke.
She whisps in through the keyhole and feels about
Like a spider's arm or a smoke-elephant's snout
Till she finds her victim.
He collapses like a balloon – she has sucked him
Empty in a flash. Her misty feeler
Blooms red as blood in water, then milkily paler –
And fades. And a hundred miles off
She disguises her burp with a laugh.

Also she has a sort of electronic
Rocket-homing trick – and that is chronic.
She steals the signature
Of whoever she wants to bewitch
And swallows it. Now wherever he might be
He sees her face, horrible with evil glee,
Hurtling at him like a rocket – WHOP!
People see him stop.
He staggers, he smooths his brow, he is astonished –
Whatever it was, it seems to have vanished.

He doesn't know what he's in for.
He's done for.

Only deep in sleep he dreams and groans
A pack of hyenas are fighting over his bones.

In a week, he dies. Then 'Goodness!' the witch says,
And yawns and falls asleep for about ten days –
Like a huge serpent that just ate
Something its own weight.

Foxgloves on the moon keep to dark caves.
They come out at the dark of the moon only and in waves
Swarm through the moon-towns and wherever there's a chink
Slip into the houses and spill all the money, clink-clink,
And crumple the notes and rearrange the silver dishes,
And dip hands into the goldfish bowls and stir the goldfishes,
And thumb the edges of mirrors, and touch the sleepers
Then at once vanish into the far distance with a wild laugh leaving the
    house smelling faintly of Virginia creepers.

Moon-Transport

Some people on the moon are so idle
They will not so much as saunter, much less sidle.

But if they cannot bear to walk, or try,
How do they get to the places where they lie?

They gather together, as people do for a bus.
'All aboard, whoever's coming with us.'

Then they climb on to each other till they are all
Clinging in one enormous human ball.

Then they roll, and so, without lifting their feet,
Progress quite successfully down the street.

Moon-Clock

Glancing at the moon-clock
Always brings a weird shock.

Somehow, somehow
It is never now.

The time is Grizzly Bear
(No time to clean your nails or do your hair)

Or the time is Oak
(Nobody's time to speak, nobody spoke)

Or the time is Rain
(Soon you'll be born and visit your grave again)

Or the time is River
(Am I here all the time or gone forever?)

Or the time is Shooting Star
(Too late to try again, stay where you are)

Or the time is still to come
And the clock's hands are stopped and its tock dumb.

Moon-Walkers

After a bad night's sleeping
All night the full moon's glare seeping
Between your closed eyelids, and you tossing and turning
With dreams of heaven burning
And cellars smoking with mystery
And erupting and debouching monsters from prehistory,

You wake with a cracking headache and eyes
Like lumps of lead, and to your intense surprise
You see all over the ceiling giant foot-tracks
Which have nothing to do with the blotches and cracks.

Enormous foot-prints of the lizard sort
Give you gooseflesh and sink you deep in thought.

So you carefully get out of bed
Ready to see your foot enclosed in an alligator-type head,

But your house is quite empty, not even a newt in a cup,
Only these giant mud-splodge claw-foot prints all over the ceilings
    wherever you look up

And all over the walls and everywhere
Over the furniture and the linen and then your hair

Really stands on end as you realise every one
Of these tramplers must have weighed at least a ton,

Nevertheless they came out like the far stars noiseless and weightless
    in the night
And vanished at first light

As if it were only the light which keeps them hid –

Or as if they came out of your dreams and went back in there (which
  they probably did).

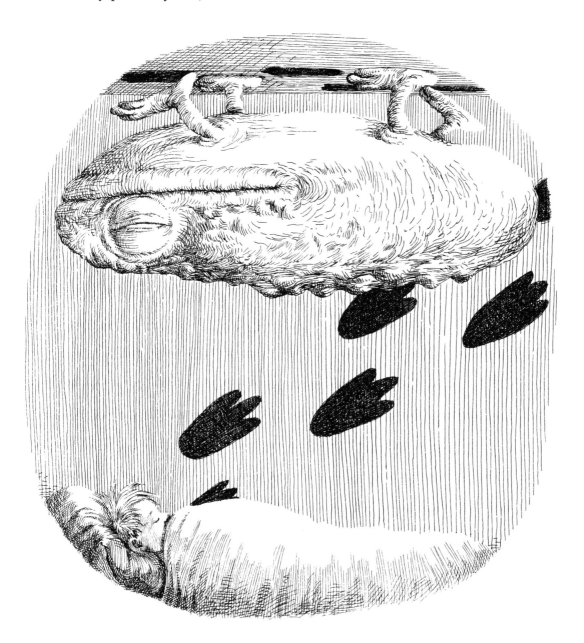

The savage tribes that have their lairs
  In the moon's extinct craters
Pray to the Earth with savage prayers:
  'O Thou who didst create us

Speak to us through our Holy bells.
  O with thy wisdom guide us.
Correct with bong of decibels
  The lunatic inside us.'

So then they swing the bells they have slung
  In each volcano's womb,
And Earth begins to declare with clung
  And clang and mumbling boom

Out of one bell: 'Towers fall
  And dunghills rise.' And from another:
'He who thinks he knows it all
  Marries his own mother.'

'Only an owl knows the worth of an owl,'
  Clanks one with a clunk.
'Let every man,' groans one in toil,
  'Skin his own skunk.'

'The head is older than the book,'
  Shrills one with sour tone,
And 'Beauty is only skin deep,
  But ugly goes to the bone.'

Then: 'He who does not swell in the warm
   Will not shrink in the cold.'
Another is muttering: 'Hair by hair
   You may pluck a tiger bald.'

'Going to ruin is silent work,'
   One dins with numbing bellow.
And: 'Love and Thirst, they know no shame,
   But the Itch beats them hollow.'

'All things, save Love and Music,
   Shall perish,' another cries.
'Downcast is King of illness.'
   'Dead fathers have huge eyes.'

So on and on the bells declare
The Word of Earth to them up there.

Singing on the Moon

Singing on the moon seems precarious.
Hum the slightest air
And some moon-monster sails up and perches to stare.
These monsters are moonily various.

If you sing in your bath
Risks are one of these monster entities
Will come crash through the wall and with dusty eyes
Perch on the taps to stare, as if in wrath.

The tenor who practises on a volcano side
Sees eyes rising over the crater rim
To fix their incredulity on him –
There is no place on the moon where a singer can hide

And not raise some such being face to face.
But do not be alarmed – their seeming fury
Comes from their passion for music being so fiery.
So if you just sing from your heart, and stay in your place,

At your song's end the monster will cry out madly
And fling down money, probably far more than you can spend,
And kiss your shoe with his horrific front-end,
Then shudder away with cries of rapture diminishing sadly.

A Moon-Hare

So I run out. I am holding a hare.
With a million terrified people I stare

From the point of Manhattan, across the Atlantic.
The skies are in flames. The people are frantic.

The moon is hurtling hugely toward
The crouching earth and its cringing horde.

Huger, and golder, and growing to shatter
Our globe of skyscrapers and water.

And I see, as it bulges and overhangs,
It is teeming with fiery, terrible things.

And I see, as it looms, it is packed to burst
With insect, fish, and bird and beast,

And the trees and the blossoms of Paradise,
And each is a miracle Paradise

Crammed with miracles. I watch it grow.
I hear earth's people screaming 'No!'

As it rolls under the glistening horizon.
Then the world-ending collision

Flings us flat. That impact jars
Us into a space with different stars.

The skyscrapers, blazed-out with the shock,
Frail as spider-web curtains they rock.

The big-eyed, up-eared hare I hold
Is solid flame of living gold.

Earth-Moon

Once upon a time there was a person
He was walking along
He met the full burning moon
Rolling slowly toward him
Crushing the stones and houses by the wayside.
He shut his eyes from the glare.
He drew his dagger
And stabbed and stabbed and stabbed.
The cry that quit the moon's wounds
Circled the earth.
The moon shrank, like a punctured airship,
Shrank, shrank, smaller, smaller,
Till it was nothing
But a silk handkerchief, torn,
And wet as with tears.
The person picked it up. He walked on
Into moonless night
Carrying this strange trophy.

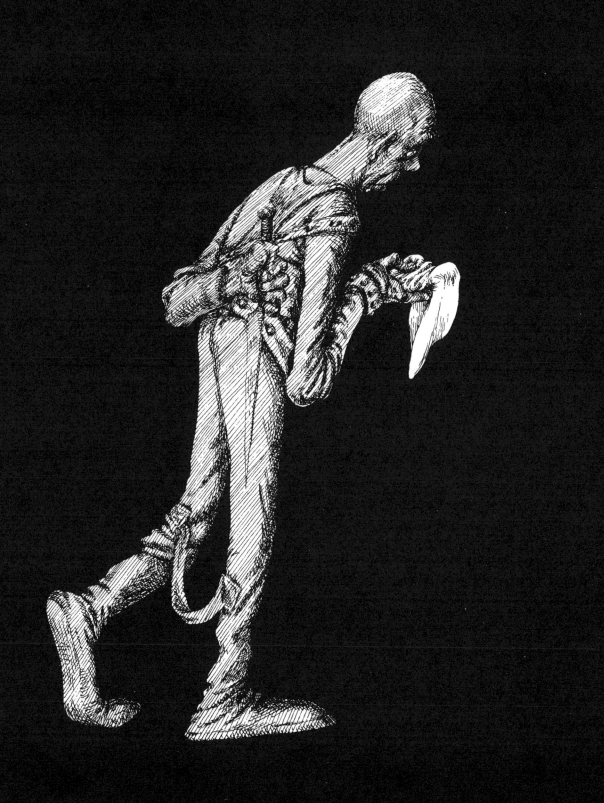